The Ultimate Self-Teaching Method!

Level 1

Audio Access Included

PLAYBACK+
Speed • Pitch • Balance • Loop

Play Viola Today!

A Complete Guide to the Basics

D0613700

To access audio visit:
www.halleonard.com/mylibrary

Enter Code
6088-2946-4741-2162

by Katy Flaccavento
Audio Arrangements and Viola Recordings by Katy Flaccavento
Produced by Zachary Gillerlain

ISBN 978-1-4950-2989-9

HAL•LEONARD®
CORPORATION
7777 W. BLUEMOUND RD. P.O. BOX 13819 MILWAUKEE, WI 53213

In Australia Contact:
Hal Leonard Australia Pty. Ltd.
4 Lentara Court
Cheltenham, Victoria, 3192 Australia
Email: ausadmin@halleonard.com.au

Visit Hal Leonard Online at
www.halleonard.com

Introduction

Track 1

Welcome to *Play Viola Today!*—the book designed to nurture your musical skills and prepare you for any style of viola playing, from classical to folk to pop. Regardless of your taste in music, *Play Viola Today!* will give you the start you need.

About the Online Audio

It's rewarding and fun to play the viola, and the accompanying online audio will make learning the viola even more enjoyable. The online audio is intended to take you step-by-step through each lesson and allows you to play each song along with full accompaniment. Much like an in-person lesson, the best way to learn the material is to first read and practice on your own, then listen to the online audio. With *Play Viola Today!* you can learn at your own pace. Whenever you do not fully understand something presented in a lesson, look to the online audio as a secondary guide. Each track has been assigned a number, so if you need to hear or practice an example again, you can find it immediately.

Contents

The Basics

Meet the Viola

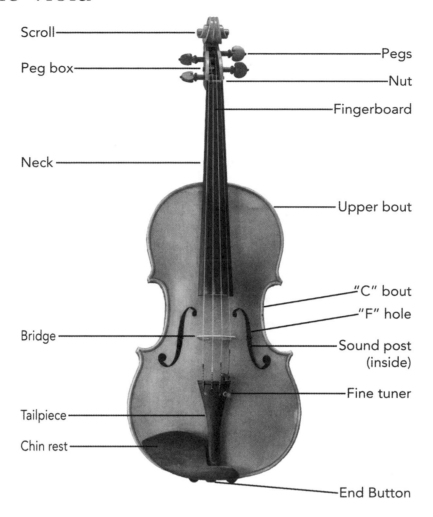

Scroll

Pegs

Peg box

Nut

Fingerboard

Neck

Upper bout

"C" bout

"F" hole

Bridge

Sound post (inside)

Fine tuner

Tailpiece

Chin rest

End Button

The Bow

Tip

Stick

Winding

Frog

Bow hair

Ferrule Screw

Before using your bow, you must do two things: tighten the bow hairs and rosin them. To tighten your bow, turn the screw clockwise, or away from you, until the hair is firm. While the bow hair should be taut, be careful not to over-tighten the hair. Make sure you can still see a slight curve in the stick part of the bow. If the stick is straight then the bow is too tight, and you will need to loosen it slightly.

After you have tightened your bow, apply rosin to the bow hair. When applying rosin, thoroughly coat the bow hair from frog to tip.

When you are done playing, before storing your bow in its case, make sure to loosen the bow hair by turning the screw toward you. Keeping the bow hair too tight for too long causes the bow hair to stretch out.

Holding the Viola

Track 2

Now it's time to pick up your instrument and learn how to properly hold it.

To begin, carefully pick your viola up by the neck, keeping the strings facing away from you. Hold the instrument close to where the neck meets the body.

Carefully bring the viola towards you with the strings now facing the ceiling. Let the viola sit between the left side of your face under your jaw and the top of your shoulder. The viola should feel like an extension of your body.

The most common mistake for a beginner is to place the chin rest under the chin rather than under the jaw on the side of your face. Although it's called a chin rest, it's your jaw that sits on the chin rest—not the chin.

A snug grip of the viola between your jaw and shoulder is what supports the weight of the viola. Avoid supporting the weight of the viola with your hand. It is important that your hand and fingers have freedom to move around on the instrument. Now that you have the viola firmly gripped

between your jaw and shoulder, bring your left hand to just about 1½" from the nut and curve your fingers around to touch the strings. A relaxed body is the key to good technique and ease of playing. Allow your thumb to loosely rest along the left side of the neck, keeping it straight but not stiff. The elbow should be directly under the middle of the viola and your wrist should remain in a straight line with your elbow. Avoid having a floppy wrist, what is known as "pancake wrist."

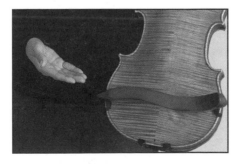

The use of a shoulder rest is strongly recommended to help make holding the viola easier and more comfortable.

Holding the viola properly requires a delicate balance of a relaxed yet sturdy grip. This will take practice and patience so don't get frustrated if it takes a while to get comfortable holding the viola.

Practice Tip: Each time you take out your viola, before doing anything else, practice supporting your viola without your left hand. The more you work on this, the more stamina you will build.

The Bow Hold

Gripping the bow properly is just as important as correctly holding the viola. Until you are comfortable holding the bow and viola together, begin by holding the bow on its own.

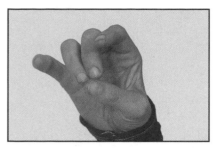

To get you prepared, we will do a quick exercise without the bow. With your right hand, make a rabbit (the kind you would make for shadow puppets). If you are doing this correctly, then your middle and ring finger will be gently slumped over your thumb, which should be slightly curved. Your pointer and pinky fingers are the rabbit ears. Let the "ears" relax into a natural, comfortable position—now you have a floppy-eared rabbit! This is basically what your hand will look like while holding the bow.

Track 4

Now, pick up the stick of your bow with your right hand. Avoid touching the hair of the bow. Touching the bow hair with your hands will cause the hair to get oily. Oily bow hair will not hold rosin; this is problemlatic because if your bow cannot hold rosin, you simply cannot make any sound.

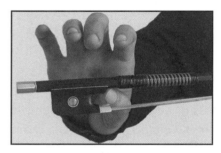

Supporting the weight of the bow with your left hand, with the bow hair facing toward the ground, place the tip of your right thumb in the area where the inside of the frog meets the stick. Keep the thumb loosely bent.

Next, still supporting the weight of the bow with your left hand, place the tip of your pinky next to the screw - the pinky should be slightly bent. The pinky and thumb are the main drivers of the bow.

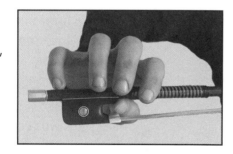

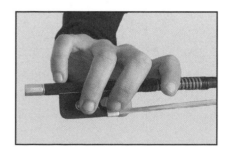

Allow your middle and ring finger to gently fall in place on the stick. Your middle two fingers should lie over the frog directly above the thumb. Last, but not least, your pointer finger should be comfortably relaxed over the winding of the stick.

Practice Tip: Hold the bow with and without support from your left hand. In lesson 5 you will work more in-depth with the bow, and you will learn exercises to strengthen your fingers, especially your pinky. These exercises are included in *Play Viola Today!* to help you improve your overall dexterity.

Tuning

Track 5

Looking at the viola with the strings facing toward you, from left to right, the four strings of the viola are tuned to the following pitches (lowest to highest): C-G-D-A

Tightening or loosening the strings by turning the pegs will change the pitch of the string. Always tune your instrument before practicing or performing.

If you are reading this book, chances are you are a beginner and your viola will have a fine tuner at least on your A string (if not all of your strings). Remember that fine tuners are located on the top end of the tailpiece and serve the purpose of getting your strings more finely tuned. Use the fine tuners only after you have done the bulk of tuning with the viola's pegs.

Track 6

To begin the tuning process, place your viola on your knee with the strings facing you. Tune your A string first by listening to the A tone on the audio track. You can also use the A pitch from a keyboard or a tuner. Listen carefully to the A pitch! If your A sounds lower than the A that you are matching, slowly turn the A string peg away from you. This will tighten the string and make the pitch higher. If your A is higher than the A tone you are matching, then you will need to lower your A. Do this by loosening the string; turning the peg toward you. Once your A is in unison with the A you are matching, your A string is in tune.

Reading Music

To indicate musical sound, we use symbols called **notes**.

For basic purposes, **pitch** is the highness or lowness of a note. At the scientific level, pitch is the frequency at which you are hearing a tone. A higher sounding pitch emits a greater number of vibrations, while a lower sounding pitch emits fewer vibrations. Pitch is visually depicted by a note's horizontal placement on the musical staff. Notes higher on the staff are higher in pitch and notes lower on the staff are lower in pitch. To give tonal order to pitches, we use the first seven letters of the alphabet: A B C D E F G. The alto clef (𝄡) assigns a certain pitch name to each line and space on the staff and is centered around the C pitch, located on the middle line of the staff.

While most viola music is written in the alto clef, it is also common to see music in a higher register written in the violin's treble clef (𝄞). To begin with, you will work only with the alto clef.

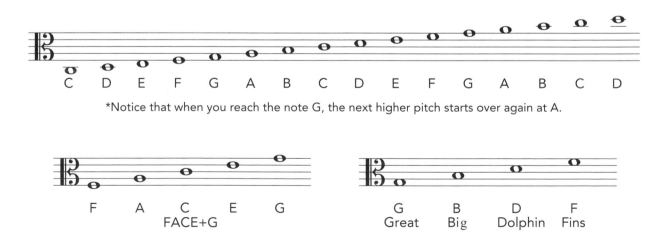

*Notice that when you reach the note G, the next higher pitch starts over again at A.

To remember the lines better use the word FACE + G. To remember the spaces use the acronym Great Big Dolphin Fins. Feel free to make up your own word association to better remember the note names of the lines and spaces.

Musical pitches are more specifically defined by their placement in a certain key signature, which is a pattern of sharps (#) or flats (♭) placed at the beginning of the staff. For example, the pitch D# will sound slightly higher than the natural D, while the D♭ will sound slightly lower than a natural D.

slightly higher than

slightly lower than

You will learn more about key signatures in later lessons. For now, we will work in the key of C, which has no sharps or flats (only naturals).

Rhythm in music can be described as the measured movement of sound through time.

At the core of rhythm is the **beat**, which is the steady and repetitive pulse that drives the notes through time. To help you keep track of the beats in a piece of music, the staff is divided into **measures** (or bars). Each measure is then separated by **bar lines**.

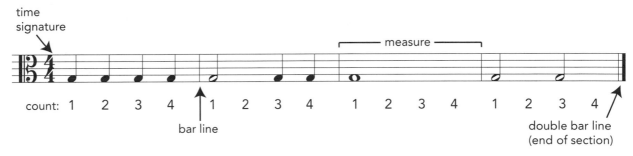

time signature

measure

count: 1   2   3   4   1   2   3   4   1   2   3   4   1   2   3   4

bar line

double bar line (end of section)

The **time signature** (or **meter**) is an important piece of rhythmic information that tells the player the number of beats in each measure. Always placed after the key signature, the time signature gives the player an idea of the "feel" of a specific piece of music.

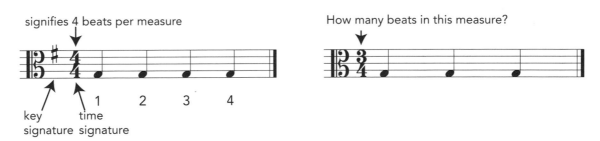

signifies 4 beats per measure

How many beats in this measure?

1   2   3   4

key signature   time signature

In the first example above you see a 4 as the top number. The top number in a time signature tells you how many beats are in each measure, while the bottom number tells you which note duration will receive the beat.

The last main rhythmic element of a note is its **duration** (or value), meaning how long or short a note is played. To depict rhythmic value, we use a few methods to slightly alter the appearance of the note. Below are the most basic note values:

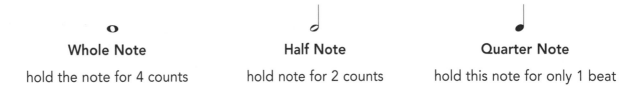

Whole Note

hold the note for 4 counts

Half Note

hold note for 2 counts

Quarter Note

hold this note for only 1 beat

Open Strings

Track 7

Now that you know more about the viola and the basics of reading music, you are ready to begin playing!

From lowest to highest, the viola strings are: C G D A.

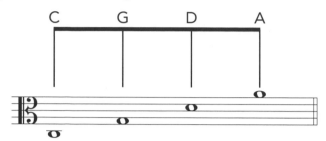

Commit the names of each open string and its corresponding position on the staff to memory. Notice that the notes associated with the open strings are contained only within the spaces. Begin without your bow and play **pizzicato** (*pizz.*). Pizzicato is an Italian word, which means "to pluck."

With your viola in proper playing position, rest your right thumb against the lower right hand corner of the fingerboard. Use your index finger to pluck each open string. As you pluck each string, starting from the lowest string, say the note name out loud while looking at its position on the staff. A relaxed, but assertive plucking motion is the key to a pleasant tone.

*Be careful not to pluck so hard that the string snaps against the fingerboard.

Pizzicato vs. Arco

There are two basic options for producing sound on the viola: **Pizzicato** (plucking) and **Arco** (using the bow). In most cases, when no instruction is given, you will use the bow (arco).

Although you will use the bow in the second half of the lesson, begin first by using *pizz.* to master the open strings.

You will notice throughout the book that many musical terms, like *pizzicato* and *arco*, are in the Italian language. Italian is the standard language for musical directions and terms. This is due largely to the fact that Italians were the first to delineate modern musical notation.

Note Names

For each exercise, say the name of every note as you play it. Pay close attention to the note's position on the staff. You can do this through the duration of the book or until you feel comfortable reading all the notes.

Open String Slow Pizz.

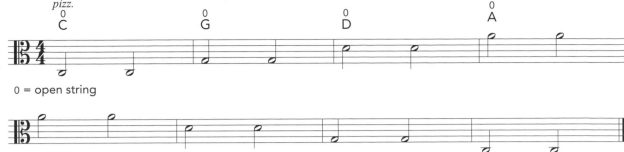

Notice the notes are all half notes. Remember that each half note should be held for 2 counts.

0 = open string

More to Pizzicato

Using the Bow

Bring the viola to the proper playing position. If you are still unsure of how to properly hold the viola, refer to page 4 from lesson 1. Remember to support the viola by holding it firmly between the jaw and left shoulder. The left hand should be free to move around and should NOT support the weight of the instrument.

Now pick up the bow with your right hand and place the bow on the G string. Make sure you are using the proper bow hold.

For the best tone production, place the bow halfway between the bridge and the fingerboard—try to keep the bow hair flat as you draw the bow across the string. With your right arm bent at a 90 degree angle, start with the bow closer to the frog, just as the photo demonstrates.

Now that the bow is carefully placed, pull the bow from your elbow down towards the floor until you reach the bow's tip. The motion of pulling the bow is called a **down-bow** and is denoted using this symbol: ⊓

Next, starting at the tip of the bow, close your arm in from your elbow and push the bow away from you until you have returned to the frog. This is called an **up-bow** and is denoted using this symbol: ∨

In the musical example "Go Bow Go," you will use the bow on each of your open strings. Use a down bow for the first half note in each measure and an up bow for the second half note in each measure.

Go Bow Go

Track 10

► Keep your bow halfway in between the bridge and the fingerboard.

As you move from one string to the next, raise and lower your arm just enough to draw your bow easily across each string.

Open String Mix Up

Track 11

Practice Check List:

- Correct viola hold - left arm is relaxed
- Proper bow grip - right arm is relaxed
- Keep bow halfway between the bridge and the fingerboard
- Bow arm slightly raised for bottom strings and slightly lowered for top strings
- Memorize open string note names
- Keep a steady quarter note beat

Open String Work Out

Track 12

You can use any of the musical examples from lesson 2 as daily warm-up exercises. For each example play *pizzicato* first, then use your bow (*arco*).

G String Notes

Before learning the new notes on the G string, use the "Open String Review" to refresh your memory on the open string notes and their position on the staff. Play the exercise *pizzicato* first and then play a second time using your bow.

Track 13

Open String Review

Track 14

New Note: A

The note A sounds a whole step above the open G. To play the new note A, place the tip of your first finger about 1½" below the nut. Always keep your fingers curved and relaxed when playing. Be careful not to let the pinky curl up under the fingerboard.

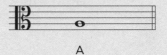

A

The diagram on the left shows each finger with an assigned number. It is important to learn the finger number that is associated with playing a certain note, i.e., the A on the G string is most commonly played with the first finger. You will see finger numbers in your music examples. These numbers serve as a further guide for playing the correct note with the proper finger. These numbers are small and will appear above the note.

left hand

Track 15

► When the number 0 appears above a note, this means to play the open string (with no fingers down).

First Finger on G

Intervals

Intervals are the distance between two pitches. In this lesson, you will learn the two smallest intervals in Western music. The best way to understand intervals is by looking at a keyboard or piano.

Half Step: the smallest distance between two notes in Western music. On a keyboard a half step is the distance from any key to the next closest key (either black or white). This is also known as a minor second.

Whole Step: this interval is composed of two half steps. The distance from your open G to your new note A is a whole step. If you look at a keyboard, a whole step is the distance between any two white keys with a black key in between (or the distance between any two keys with a key in between them). The whole step is also called a major second.

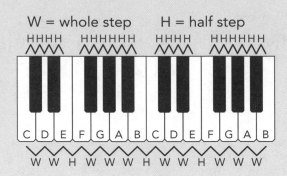

While playing the exercise below, "First Finger Hop," concentrate on hearing the whole step between the open G and the new note A. In practicing the placement of your first finger, you are gaining muscle memory. Eventually, once you place your finger in the same place enough times, your finger will know where to go automatically.

Track 16

First Finger Hop

Track 17

New Note: B

The new note B is also one whole step away from first finger A. Place finger number two about 1¼" from finger one to play new note B. Remember to keep your fingers curved and relaxed. Any tension in your arm, hand, or fingers not only negatively effects tone production, but can also cause pain during playing.

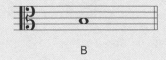

B

To improve your **intonation**, or accuracy of pitch, use a combination of your ear and the online audio. You can also match pitches using a keyboard or a digital tuner.

Track 18

Second Finger Stroll

Begin by plucking first and playing the notes slowly. Once you feel confident with the rhythm and your finger placement, play the example more quickly.

Track 19

Two Finger Rhythm Challenge

Play "Hot Cross Buns" *pizzicato* first, then pick up your bow and play it a second time *arco*.

Track 20

Hot Cross Buns

Once you are comfortable playing "Hot Cross Buns" both *pizz.* and *arco*, go back to the previous songs in this lesson and play them all *arco* (with the bow).

Track 21

Rests

Rests are symbols used to indicate beats of silence.

Quarter Rest: equals one beat of silence (just as a quarter note equals one beat of sound).

Half Rest: two beats of silence - the same duration as a half note.

Whole Rest: four beats of silence - the same duration as a whole note. In the case of a song in 4/4 time, a whole rest means a full measure of silence.

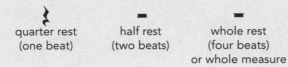

quarter rest   half rest   whole rest
(one beat)   (two beats)   (four beats)
                                      or whole measure

"Resting Song" focuses on reading the three basic rest symbols. You will see that the half rest and whole rest look similar. You can distinguish them by their position within the staff. The half rest sits above the middle line of the staff, while the whole rest sits underneath the fourth line.

Track 22

Resting Song

Notice the two dots at the end of "Mary's Little Lamb" (next to the double bar line). This is a **repeat sign**, which means go back to the beginning of the song and play through it a second time.

Track 23

Mary's Little Lamb

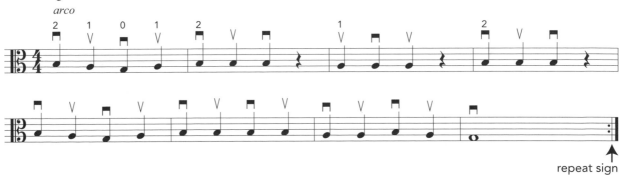

13

Track 24

New Note: C

So far, you have learned notes that sound a whole step apart from each other. The new note, third finger C, however, is only a half step away from the second finger note B. To play C, place your third finger directly next to your second finger (they should almost touch). Remember to keep your fingers curved and your arm tension-free.

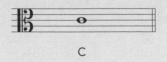

C

To help you tonally recognize a half step, think of the *Jaws* movie theme.

Track 25

► This example uses fingers 2 and 3 only. Begin with 2 on the G string.

Halloween Half Step

play *pizz.*, then play *arco*

With the G String notes and open D, you can now play a five note scale. Keep all three of your fingers down on the G string while crossing over to play the open D. This way, when you are ready to go back to the notes on the G string, your fingers will already to be in place.

Track 26

Five Note Scale

play *pizz.*, then play *arco*

keep finger 3 down

Lift and Breathe

In the musical example below, you will notice commas above certain rests. For a wind player, this symbol means to take a breath or pause. For the string player, it means you will lift your bow (you should also use this time to take a breath). In measure 4, you will see a note with a down bow, followed by a comma over top of a rest. Pull the bow from frog to tip, lift the bow, then return the bow back to the frog, or starting point, for the second down bow. Because the bow lift motion forms a circle in the air, it is also referred to as a **circle bow**.

"Jingle Bells" uses notes on the G string as well as the open D string.

Track 27

► Notice the two breath marks (commas) and remember to lift your bow when you see them.

Jingle Bells

D String Notes

Before learning the new notes on the D string, use the theme from Dvořák's *New World Symphony* to refresh your memory on the G string notes and their position on the staff.

Track 28

New World Theme

Antonin Dvořák

► Notice the repeat sign! Remember to go back to the beginning and play again.

Track 29

New Note: E

Place your first finger about 1½" below the nut on the D string to sound the new note E. Notice that your finger is in the same place to play first finger E (on the D string) as it was to play first finger B (on the G string). As you have with previous notes, use the audio examples to help you match the pitch of the new note E.

E

Track 30

Whole Step Hoedown

arco

For the example below you will use the open G and first finger A as well as open D and the new note—first finger E. Remember to shift your bow arm up slightly when playing the G string and down slightly when playing the D string. When crossing from one string to the next, take your time and set the bow firmly on the string before drawing it.

Track 31

First Finger Fitness

arco

Track 32

New Note: F♯

As you learned in lesson 1, placing a sharp on the staff before any given note raises that note by a half step. If you think about a note in terms of its frequency, an F♯ will vibrate at a slightly faster frequency than an F natural, thus making the F♯ sound slightly higher in pitch. The second finger F♯ is one whole step above the first finger E. To play F♯, place your second finger 1¼" above your first finger on the D string.

F♯

Accidentals

Accidentals are symbols that modify the pitch of a note. A pitch modified by an accidental is NOT a member of the scale indicated by the song's key signature. Accidentals come in three forms: sharp(♯), natural(♮), and flat(♭).

In the example below, notice that the F♯ is written as an accidental.

Track 33

Accidental F

keep bow on string,
but do not move it

Key Signature

In the simplest terms, a **key signature** denotes whether pitches should be played as sharp(♯), natural(♮), and flat(♭) throughout an entire piece. The first key signature you will learn is G major. G major contains all natural notes with the exception of the note F, which is an F♯. The key signature is always identified at the beginning of a piece and is placed directly before the time signature.

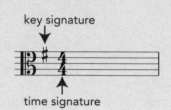

key signature

time signature

Notice the key signature now directly in front of the time signature. Remember that the F in the key of G major is sharp, which means your second finger is one whole step apart from your first finger. Now that the key is identified as having an F♯, the F♯ is no longer notated as an accidental.

Track 34

► Don't forget to keep your left arm relaxed (not lazy) and your bow arm tension-free.

1s and 2s

As you play more and learn new notes, ask yourself these questions:

- Am I holding the weight of the instrument with my jaw and shoulder? Check this by dropping your left hand away from the instrument to see if you are able to hold your instrument without the aid of your hand.
- Am I driving the bow mostly with my pinky and thumb?
- Am I gripping the bow loosely?

If you feel tension in either your left or right arm, stop playing, put your bow and/or instrument down, relax, and then pick up your bow and/or instrument after a short break.

New Note: G

The new note G sounds a half step higher than F♯. Again, the half step is a smaller distance between notes than a whole step. To play G on the D string place your third finger directly next to your second finger—your fingers should barely touch. Keep your fingers curved and relaxed. Your pinky should be hovering over the fingerboard and not curled under the fingerboard.

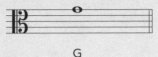

G

For "Half-Stepping to G" begin with all 3 fingers down on the D string. This will make it easier to play the second finger F♯ following the third finger G.

Half-Stepping to G

An **etude** is a musical study, typically an instrumental composition, which is designed to provide practice material for honing a certain technical skill. Use the etude below to help you practice all of the D string notes. Practice slowly at your own pace. Once you feel more confident playing the example, practice along with audio track.

D String Etude

The Scale

A **scale** is a series of ascending or descending notes, positioned in alphabetical order. The type of scale is determined by whether the interval between each scale degree is a whole step (W) or a half step (H). The arrangement of intervals for a major scale is W W H W W W H.

When you begin on the note G and follow this pattern, the scale has one sharp – F♯. The G major scale is the first of three scales you will learn in this book.

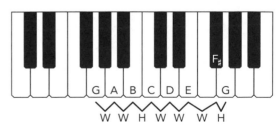

17

Track 38

G Major Scale

G Major Double Up

Track 39

► Try to keep a steady and even quarter note beat.

The following example, "London Bridge," is written in the key of G major and uses the G major scale pattern. Remember to keep your second finger apart from your first on both the G and D strings.

London Bridge

Track 40

New Intervals: Perfect Fourth and Fifth

As stated in lesson 3, an interval is the distance between any two pitches. You have already learned the half step (minor second) and the whole step (major second).

Perfect Fourth: any two notes separated by four places on a staff. The perfect fourth is composed of five half steps, or semi-tones. The first two notes in the song "Here Comes the Bride" is a great example of the perfect fourth interval.

Perfect Fifth: The viola's open strings are tuned using the interval of the fifth. From bottom to top (C, G, D, A) each string is a fifth apart. The perfect fifth interval is separated by five places on the staff and is composed of seven half steps or three and a half steps. The beginning of "Twinkle, Twinkle Little Star" is one musical example of the perfect fifth interval.

"Fantastic Fourths" requires you to go directly from the open string to your third finger. When playing the third finger, keep your first and second fingers down as well.

Fantastic Fourths

Track 41

► Take your time and play slowly so that you can get the jumps from the open string note to the third finger.

It is a common misconception that the classical composer Mozart is responsible for the creation of "Twinkle, Twinkle Little Star." The melody comes from an old French folk song and became later known as "Twinkle, Twinkle Little Star" after London poets Jane and Anne Taylor borrowed the theme for their nursery rhyme "The Star." While Mozart did not compose the main melody, he did create several variations on this general theme.

Twinkle, Twinkle

Track 42

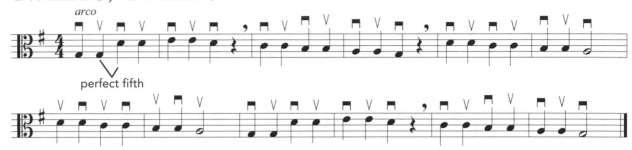

The **Air** is an accompanied solo song, which saw great success during the late 16th and early 17th centuries. Touting characteristics of grace and elegance, the typical Air dealt with subjects of romance and was often strophic, meaning each stanza contained the same music. Play "Air in G Major" *arco*. If necessary, play *pizzicato* first to practice the notes before adding the bow.

Air in G Major

Track 43

Working on the Bow

Proper bow technique is crucial to producing the best tone possible, thus this lesson focuses on making you more comfortable with your bow.

For the first half of this lesson, you will work exclusively with your bow. You will not need to pick up your viola until the second part of lesson 5.

Track 44

Bow Hold Review

- Tip of thumb is placed in the area where the inside of the frog meets the stick—thumb is loosely bent.

- Pinky is curved and tip is placed next to the screw—the pinky drives the bow.

- Middle two fingers are lightly curved over the frog and sit directly above the thumb; they just relax and enjoy the ride.

- The outside part of your index finger's knuckle rests gently over the winding of the stick. Be careful not to curl your first finger around the stick.

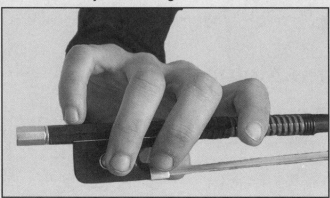

Check your bow grip before attempting any of the bow-hold exercises. For now, keep your viola in its case and use the bow exercises to warm-up your bow hand separately. Practicing these exercises daily will improve your bow technique and make you more comfortable with the proper bow grip.

Track 45

The Bow Hold Exercises

Bow exercises are designed to make your bow arm, hand, and fingers strong and agile. For each of the following exercises, until you are comfortable with the bow, reduce the weight of the bow by holding it farther up the stick, away from the frog. When you want to practice your bow hand technique, but you are not near your bow, you can practice these exercises on other objects, such as a pencil or toothbrush.

As you complete the bow exercises below, be sure to take breaks so your hand does not get fatigued or tense. If your hand is feeling cramped or tired, stop the exercise, put your bow down, and shake out your hand. Once your hand has returned to a relaxed state, pick up the bow and continue working.

Finger Pushups

Begin by lifting the index finger off of the stick and then placing it back on the stick. Then press down slightly on the stick. Next, lift your middle finger, and then place it back in its original position. Continue by lifting your ring finger, then return it gently to its place on the frog. Finally, lift your pinky finger high off the stick. After returning it the pinky back to the area near the screw, push down slightly with your pinky. This exercise is designed to strengthen your fingers and to train each finger to operate independently.

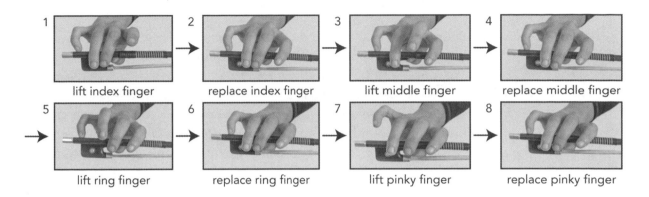

| 1 lift index finger | 2 replace index finger | 3 lift middle finger | 4 replace middle finger |
| 5 lift ring finger | 6 replace ring finger | 7 lift pinky finger | 8 replace pinky finger |

Wave Bye-Bye

Using the motion only in your wrist, wave goodbye while holding the bow with the proper grip.

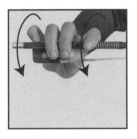 

Windshield Wipers

Using the proper bow grip, hold you bow straight up and down. Next, rotate your forearm to create a "windshield wiper" motion.

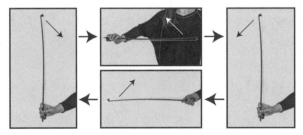

Extend and Retract

Start with your fingers curved and with the proper bow grip. Slowly straighten your fingers and thumb at the same time—do not lock your fingers. Then, slowly curl your fingers back up to the proper bow grip. Repeat this extend/retract motion several times.

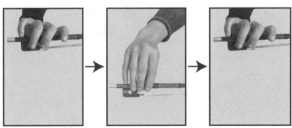

Track 46

Now that you have warmed up your bow hand, pick up your viola. The second part of lesson 5 focuses on drawing and driving a straight bow. You will use only open strings to practice drawing the bow so that you can pay close attention to your bow arm.

Drawing a Straight Bow

Drawing a straight and controlled bow is a key ingredient to producing a beautiful and pleasing tone on the viola. Beginners have a tendency to draw the bow arm behind the body rather than in front, which causes the bow to be drawn diagonally across the strings instead of straight across the strings. While it seems easier at first to use your entire arm to push and pull the bow, focus on using the lower part of the arm to drive the bow. Think of the elbow as a hinge, with the lower part of your arm connected to the hinge. The top of your arm will remain still while the lower part of your arm moves fluidly to push and pull the bow. Remember that for the down bow, your arm will open in a downward motion toward the ground. To complete the up bow motion, close your arm in from the elbow pushing your bow toward the ceiling. Keep your wrist loose and tension-free.

Use the long open string whole notes in the exercise below to practice drawing a straight bow. Begin by practicing in the mirror. Focus solely on your bow hand and arm and watch your bow in the mirror as you draw it. Make sure your bow remains parallel to the bridge as you draw it from frog to tip. Keep the bow between the bridge and fingerboard to keep the tone of your instrument confident, yet warm.

Track 47

Bow Arm Ballad

While you are watching what a straight bow looks like, try to also think about what drawing a straight bow feels like. By doing this, you will build muscle memory. Once you form muscle memory in your bow arm, you will not have to think about the proper motion. For "Bow in Line," you will need to draw your bow faster, while still keeping it straight and in between the bridge and fingerboard.

Track 48

Bow in Line

Practice Tip: If you are having trouble keeping the top part of your arm still while drawing the bow, try pressing your shoulder against a door frame and then draw the bow. This will ensure that you are only drawing the bow from the elbow down.

Lesson 6 | A String Notes

Congratulations on getting through the first half of *Play Viola Today!* Now that you have successfully completed the first five lessons of the book and taken some time to work on the bow and instrument individually, it's time to learn new notes on the A string. Before you begin on the A string, take about ten minutes to warm up and review the D string and G string notes.

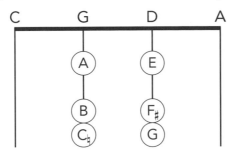

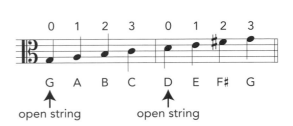

Track 49

G Major Scale Warm-Up

▶ Use a long bow stroke for each half note.

Track 50

Hop, Skip, and Jump

play *pizz.*, then play *arco*

Track 51

New Note: B

To learn the new note B, place your first finger about 1½" below the nut on the A string (if the strings of the instrument are facing toward you, the A string is the right-most string). The new note B sounds one whole step higher than the open A string. Continue to familiarize yourself with the sound of the whole step.

B

In the exercise below, listen carefully to the difference between the open A string and the new note B. As you have in the previous lessons, keep your stance poised and your viola and bow hold tension free.

Track 52

From A to B

pizz.

For the next exercise, try using shorter bow strokes, so that you are able to keep up with the quick tempo.

Track 53

➤ Notice the *pizz.* followed by *arco.* You must hold the bow in your hand while plucking so that you can quickly switch from *pizz.* to playing with the bow.

First Finger Jam

1st time pizz.
2nd time arco

Track 54

New Note: C♯

The new note C♯ sounds one whole step above the note B. Keep in mind that the note C natural, which you have already learned as the open C string and as third finger on the G string, is not the same note as C♯. To play C♯ on the A string, place your second finger about 1¼" below your first finger.

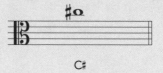

C♯

In the following music example, notice the arrow pointing upwards with a 2 next to it. This denotes that the second finger is placed apart from the first finger—also called "High 2." When a pattern contains fingers that are separated from each other, this is referred to as an open position. Thus far, you have only learned "High 2," or open position. You will learn "Low 2" and closed position in lesson 8.

Track 55

➤ Notice the time signature is in 2 rather than 4. This means only 2 beats per measure.

Slow Two

Track 56

New Note: D

To play the new note D, place your third finger directly next to your second finger on the A string. The note D, three fingers down on the A string, sounds only a half step higher than the second finger C♯. Think *Jaws* movie theme!

While the open D string and third finger D on the A string are not exactly the same notes, they are very closely related. The distance from the lower D to the next higher D (located on the A string) creates the **octave** interval. You will learn more about octaves in the following lesson.

D

Play the next exercise, "Delightful Ds," slowly and on your own without the audio track until you are comfortable making the jump from no fingers down (open A string), to three fingers down on the A string (new note D). When playing third finger D, make sure all of your fingers are down on the fingerboard alongside your third finger. Keep in mind the proper finger placement as illustrated below.

Incorrect Finger Placement

Correct Finger Placement

Track 57

Delightful Ds

D Major Scale

In lesson 4, you learned about scales and, more specifically, how to play your first scale—G major. While the G major scale contains only one sharp, F♯, the D major scale includes two sharps, F♯ and C♯. Just as the G major scale begins and ends on the note G, the D major scale begins and ends on the note D. Most scales are named after their **tonic**, or first scale degree.

D Major Scale

Track 58

D Major Double Up

Track 59

Dvořák (1841-1904) is a prolific Czech composer from the Romantic period of music. During the early to mid 1890s, Dvořák spent time in the United States, serving as the Director of The National Conservatory of Music. Dvořák was heavily influenced by the Native American music and African American spirituals he encountered while in the United States. His *New World Symphony*, commissioned by the New York Philharmonic, premiered at Carnegie Hall in 1893 and clearly reflected the new and exciting genres of music that Dvořák experienced while abroad in the States. To this day, Dvořák's *New World Symphony* is a favorite in the symphony genre and is played in orchestras frequently all around the world.

Theme from New World Symphony

Antonin Dvořák

Track 60

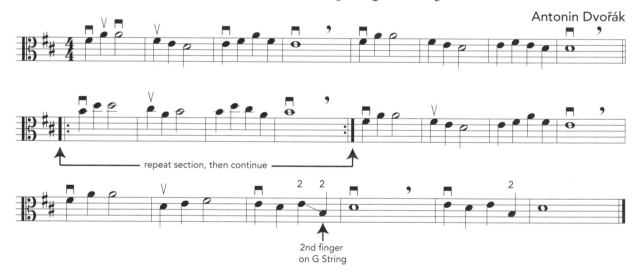

repeat section, then continue

2nd finger
on G String

Lesson 7 | C String Notes

One feature that distinguishes the viola from the violin is the C string; the C string sounds a fifth lower than the lowest string (the G string) on the violin.

Notice how thick the C string is in comparison to the G, D, and A strings. A thicker string generates lower tones, while a thinner string creates higher tones. Along with having a larger body, the thicker and lower strings contribute to the viola's distinctly mellow traits.

Track 61

New Note: D

The note D sounds a whole step higher than the open C string. Place finger 1 on the C string about 1½" below the nut. The first finger D is an octave below open D. Remember to keep your elbow forward and fingers curved.

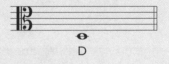

In the most traditional sense, the **serenade** is a musical work that is written and/or performed in a particular person's honor. From the Italian word **sereno**, meaning calm, the serenade is typically gentle and relaxed.

Track 62

C String Serenade

1st time pizz.
2nd time arco

Track 63

New Note: E

The note E sounds a whole step higher than D. To play E, place finger 2 about 1¼" from your first finger.

In "Wonderland Waltz," notice the time signature. How many beats are in each measure?

Track 64

Wonderland Waltz

Practice is a crucial part of mastering an instrument; so, play the etude below several times until you become comfortable with playing every note. Notice that the etude uses notes on both the G and C strings.

Track 65

Low Notes Etude

Tempo Marking

Tempo is the rate at which a piece of music is played and is usually indicated by Italian terms such as:

Adagio: slow   **Andante:** walking pace   **Allegro:** fast

Largo: very slow   **Moderato:** moderate

If you have a metronome, you will see that each of these tempo markings is identified with corresponding numbers i.e., Allegro is between 124 and 160 beats per minute (bpm).

Practicing with a metronome is very useful for becoming consistent when playing in a given tempo. Set the metronome to the number that matches the tempo marking in the music you are practicing and use the clicks of the metronome to help you stay in the proper tempo.

Pick-up Note

Also known as the **upbeat** or **anacrusis**, the **pick-up** is the note or set of notes that appear before the first full measure. Thus the measure containing the pick-up note is referred to as the pick-up measure. The sum of the beats in the final measure and the pick-up note or notes will equal a complete measure.

Track 66

Oh Susannah

Allegro

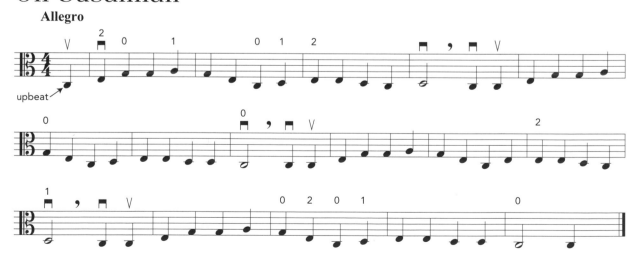

upbeat

New Note: F♮

The new note F♮ (or F natural), not to be confused with F#, sounds one half step above the second finger E on the C string. To play F♮, place finger number three directly next to your second finger—your second and third fingers should almost touch.

Aunt Rhody

Moderato

C Major Scale

You have already learned 2 scales—D Major and G Major. Now, you are ready to play a third scale, C Major. While the D Major scale contains two sharps and the G Major scale contains one sharp, the C Major scale contains no sharps (or flats). Begin by playing the open C string, then follow with your first, second, and third fingers. Next play the open G string followed by fingers one through three.

C Major Scale

Andante

Double Duty

Moderato

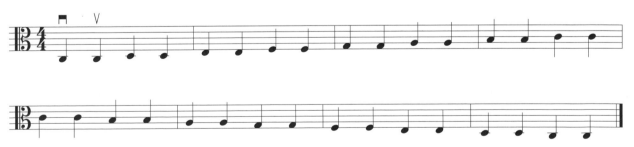

The Octave

You have learned four types of intervals—the half step, the whole step, the fifth, and the fourth. The **octave** is the interval between a musical pitch and the next closest pitch with the same note name, i.e., open C and third finger C on the G string. The interval of the octave is separated by 8 pitch degrees and is achieved when the frequency of vibrations of a note is either doubled or cut in half. Examine both exercises below. Can you identify the measures in which the octave interval occurs?

Track 71

The Octave Hop
Moderato

Airs are often very song-like, lyrical compositions. The "Scottish Air," also known as "Annie Laurie," will present you not only with interval challenges, but also new, more difficult bowings. Notice the measures that contain two up-bows in a row. Remember to use only part of the bow for the first half note up-bow, saving the remainder of the bow for the second up-bow quarter note. To get comfortable with the new bowing, practice the measures containing the double up-bows separately.

Track 72

Scottish Air
Adagio

A New Position: Low 2

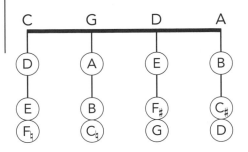

Thus far, you have used the same finger pattern on all four strings. As the illustration shows to the left, you have played only in an open second finger position, in which fingers 1 and 2 are separate, while the second and third fingers are slightly touching. By this time, you should be comfortable playing this basic finger pattern on all four strings.

Now that you know the basic finger pattern well, it is time to familiarize yourself with a new position—the closed second finger on the D and A strings. In the illustration to the right, notice the difference in the finger patterns on the C and G strings versus the D and A strings. In the new position, rather than being separate, the first and second fingers touch on the D and A string—but only on the A and D string.

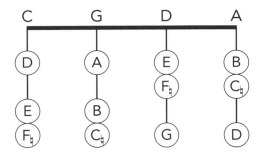

Track 73

New Note: F♮

In lesson 4, you learned the note F♯ (second finger apart from first finger on the D string). The new note F♮ sounds one half step lower than F♯, and is played by placing finger 2 directly next to finger 1 on the D string. To play the new note F♮, begin by placing your first finger on the D string. Once you are confident in the placement of your first finger, place your second finger directly next to it. Fingers 1 and 2 should touch slightly.

F

Practice Tip: Use a keyboard or tuner to check on and improve the accuracy of your pitch. You can use either of these tools to ensure that your first finger E, for example, is correct before placing your second finger to play the new note F♮.

The **lament**, found in both music and poetry, is born from an expression of grief and/or mourning. As you play "Low Finger Lament," listen for the melancholy sound.

Track 74

Low Finger Lament

Adagio

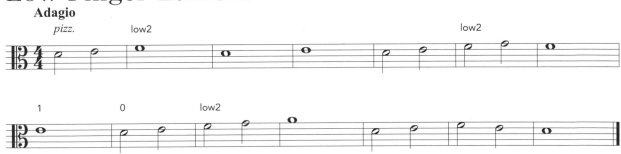

In "High and Low," you will encounter both F♯ (high 2) and F♮ (low 2). Play the exercise slowly and on your own first. Pay close attention to whether your second finger belongs next to your first finger or apart from it.

Track 75

High and Low

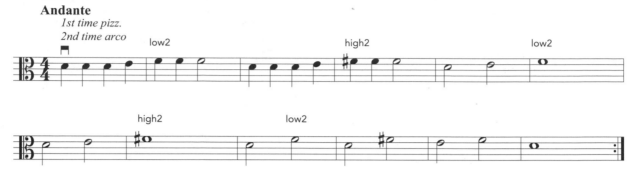

Major vs. Minor Key

Up until now, you have played only in major keys. To a Western listener, **Major Keys** produce music that sounds joyous, light-hearted, celebratory, cheery, and bright. **Minor Keys**, on the other hand, sound melancholy, somber, haunting, menacing, or dark to the Western ear.

Theoretically, the difference between the major and minor sound depends upon the intervals between each note in a particular scale. The two keyboards below show the C major scale and the A Minor scale—notice the different interval patterns.

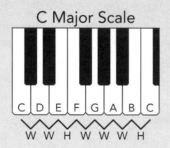
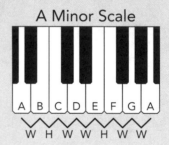

To exemplify the difference between the major and minor sound, let's revisit Dvořák's "New World Symphony Theme." You will play two versions—the first will use the new note F♮ (low 2) and the second will be the original version with an F♯ (high 2). Notice that in the first example, playing a low 2 creates a somber sound, while in the second example the use of the high second finger instead evokes a celebratory feeling.

New World Theme in Minor

► Begin with your first 2 fingers down on the string before drawing the bow.

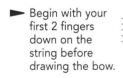

Original New World Theme (Major)

Practice Checklist

- Proper viola and bow hold

- Body is relaxed – viola and bow should feel more like a natural extension of your body. Don't forget to breathe!

- You have glanced over your music and noted the following: Key signature, time signature, tempo, bowings, finger patterns, and accidentals.

Playing low 2 on the D string does not always mean you are playing in a minor key. In the example below, "Merry Widow," you will play low 2, but will be in the key of C major.

Track 76

▶ Notice the ¾ time signature. Remember this means 3 beats per measure.

Merry Widow

Track 77

New Note: C♮

You already know how to play open string C♮ as well as C♮ on the G string (third finger). Now, you will learn a third version of C♮—low second finger on the A string. Play the new note C♮ by placing your second finger directly next to your first finger on the A string.

Play the next examples through twice—*pizz.* first time, then *arco.* Use the practice checklist included in this lesson to assist in playing new and more challenging music examples.

Track 78

Side by Side

Before playing "Bingo," take a minute to survey the notes included. Notice that you play high 2 (F#) on the D string and low 2 (C♮) on the A string. Watch for the identifiers above the second finger notes for guidance.

Track 79

Bingo

Major 3rd and Minor 3rd Intervals

Remember that an interval is the distance between two notes.

The **major 3rd interval** consists of four half-steps or two whole steps. The major 3rd interval occurs naturally between the first and third note of all major scales. In the D major scale, for example, the distance between open D and F# (high 2) is a major 3rd.

The **minor 3rd interval** consists of only three half-steps and occurs naturally between the first and third note of all minor scales. The distance between open D and F♮ (low 2) is an example of a minor 3rd.

The best way to understand the contrast between the major and minor 3rd intervals is to hear the difference. To demonstrate the difference between the major and minor 3rd, the example below uses the jump from 0 (open string) to high and low 2 on both the D and A string.

Track 80

Planet of the 3rds

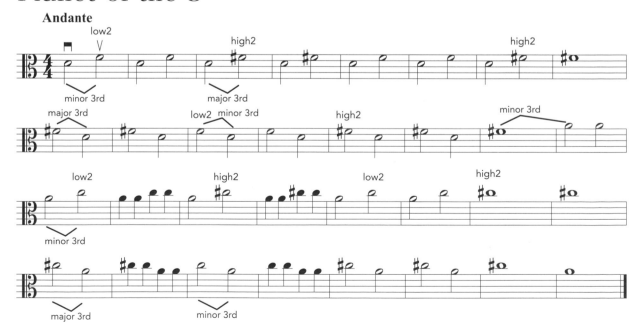

Two-Octave C Scale

Now that you have learned low 2 on the D and A strings, it's time to learn your first two-octave scale. Rather than playing only 8 notes, you will now play 15 consecutive notes, beginning with the open C and ending on second finger C♮ on the A string. Remember that the key of C major contains no sharps or flats, thus the finger pattern on the C and G string uses high 2, while the pattern on the D and A string uses low 2.

Two-Octave C Major Scale

Track 81

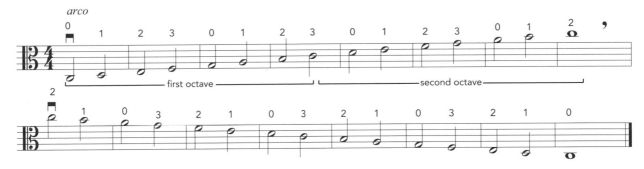

Spanning the gap between the Classical and Romantic periods in music, Beethoven (1770-1827) is one of the most notable composers in music history. Despite being deaf, Beethoven was able to create some of the most beautiful and lyrical music ever written.

German Dance

Track 82

Beethoven

Lesson 9 | Focus on Rhythm

You have already learned the most basic rhythms including the whole note (𝅝), the half note (𝅗𝅥), and the quarter note (𝅘𝅥). In this lesson, you will work mostly on furthering your rhythm skills by learning new note values and rhythmic notations. To keep you focused on rhythm, most of this lesson's examples will involve clapping or playing only on open strings.

Counting

It's typical to teach a beginning music student the method of foot-tapping to help them count the beat. While foot-tapping might seem helpful to some students in the beginning, in the long run, it's a detrimental crutch that often causes the player to fall behind the beat. Ultimately, this habit must be unlearned. Therefore, rather than learn to keep the beat externally with your foot, you will learn how to internalize the beat by counting silently in your head and by learning to subdivide the beat. Using a metronome frequently during practice is also strongly recommended as a helpful tool in building a solid internal sense of the beat.

The exercise below consists only of the rhythms you know currently. As a warm-up, clap the rhythms in the example. Make sure to count a steady four in your head, while you clap. Use the audio track included to help guide you through the exercise.

Track 83

Clapping Warm-up

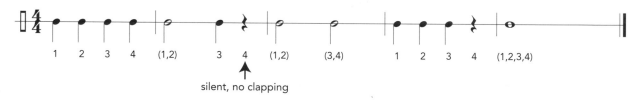

The Eighth Note

The **eighth note** (𝅘𝅥𝅮) sounds for exactly half the duration of a quarter note. Thus, two eighth notes are equal to one quarter note (𝅘𝅥). When multiple eighth notes occur in a row, they are beamed together in groups of either 2 or 4 (𝅘𝅥𝅮𝅘𝅥𝅮 or 𝅘𝅥𝅮𝅘𝅥𝅮𝅘𝅥𝅮𝅘𝅥𝅮). Because the viola speaks more slowly than its smaller violin sibling, make sure your eighth note bow strokes are quick and do not fall behind the beat. You will need to anticipate the beat while playing eighth notes.

Listen to the rhythmic example provided below—do not play it yet. Can you hear the eighth notes versus the quarter notes?

Track 84

Hearing Eighth Notes

Subdivision

Track 85

The best way to improve your understanding of, and comfort with, playing eighth notes is to learn the technique of **subdivision**. To **subdivide** means to break a larger rhythmic unit down into smaller segments. To count eighth notes using subdivision, begin by cutting the quarter note beat into two half beats. The first half of each beat will be assigned the numbers 1-4, while the second half of the beat will be counted as the ampersand (&).

In the example below, put your instrument and bow down and focus solely on learning the new eighth note rhythms. Say the count aloud: 1 & 2 & 3 & 4 & while clapping the rhythms below. Once you are comfortable clapping the example, count, 1 & 2 & 3 & 4 & silently in your head.

Clapping with Eighth Notes

Track 86

Notice in the following exercise that you are in ¾ time. Since there are only 3 beats instead of 4, the subdivision count for this time signature is 1 & 2 & 3 &.

Clapping in 3/4

Track 87

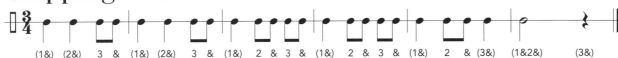

Now for the next exercise, pick up your instrument and play *pizz.* followed by *arco*. Notice that you are only playing on open strings. Remember to use shorter bow strokes when playing eighth-note rhythms.

Eighth Note Study

Track 88

The Eighth Rest

The **eighth rest** ( ) is the silent counterpart to the eighth note. An eighth rest is equal to the value of an eighth note. Two eighth rests are equal to the value of one quarter rest.

In the example below, you are presented with both the eighth note and the eighth rest. Do not forget to subdivide throughout the entire exercise. This will help keep you in rhythm, especially when presented with smaller rhythmic values such as the eighth note and rest.

Short and Sweet

Track 89

Tie

Tie: a musical symbol shaped as a curved line, which connects two notes of the same pitch and name. Notes connected by a tie are played as one single note. For example, a quarter note tied to another quarter note will be held for two full beats.

The Tied Up Hoedown

Track 90

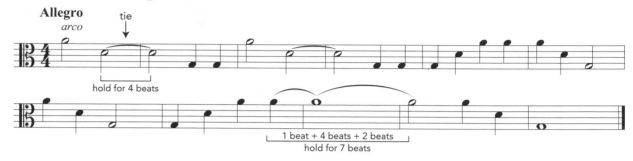

If you need help counting and keeping a steady beat, use your metronome. You can start with a slow click and then gradually increase the click tempo until you are playing the exercises quickly and effortlessly.

The Dotted Note

A **Dotted Note** occurs when a dot is added to any basic unit of rhythm. Adding one dot to a note increases that note's duration by half of the original note's value. Essentially, the dot acts in a similar fashion as the tie in that it extends the duration of the note.

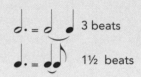

In the next example, pay close attention to the duration of each dotted note.

Dotted Dance

Track 91

Now, it's time to put all of your new rhythmic knowledge to use! You will see eighth notes, tied notes, and dotted notes in the C Major Scale below. This is also a challenge, as you will play notes in the full two-octave range of C major.

C Major 2 Octave Review

Track 92

Musicality: Putting It All Together

Congratulations for reaching the final lesson of *Play Viola Today!* Up until now you have focused mostly on the technical aspects of playing the viola. In this last lesson, you will work more specifically on musicality. Musicality is the sensitivity to performing the notes, which enhances the delivery of the notes on the page. Musicality is about going beyond just the simple notes on the page and bringing the music to life.

Track 93

Dynamics

In music, **dynamics** refer to the volume of a given note or group of notes. Playing music at varying volumes makes the music more dimensional and dynamic—hence the term dynamics. Below are the basic dynamics with their associated symbols.

piano (*p*) means soft in Italian   *forte* (*f*) means loud in Italian

The word *mezzo* in Italian means medium.

mezzo piano (*mp*) = medium soft, or slightly louder than piano

mezzo piano (*mf*) = medium loud, or slightly quieter than forte

The suffix *–issimo*, when added to a dynamic, means more of that dynamic.

pianissimo (*pp*) = more quiet, or quieter than piano

fortissimo (*ff*) = more loud, or louder than forte

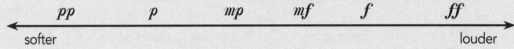

| *pp* | *p* | *mp* | *mf* | *f* | *ff* |

softer ←——————————————————————————→ louder

In "Scarborough Fair," pay close attention to the dynamic markings. For softer notes, try to draw the bow closer to your fingerboard. For louder notes, play closer to the bridge. For medium volume notes, keep the bow directly in between the fingerboard and the bridge.

Track 94

Scarborough Fair

English Folk Song

"Scarborough Fair" is written in the key of A minor. A minor has the exact same key signature as C major (no sharps or flats); however, notice that it sounds somber rather than bright and cheery.

Shading

Another form of dynamic articulation is called **shading**, in which the volume across a set of notes is gradually increased or decreased. To identify moments of shading in music, the terms **crescendo** and **decrescendo** are used.

Crescendo means to increase the volume and is symbolized with

Decrescendo, or diminuendo, is the opposite of crescendo and means to gradually decrease the volume. The symbol for decrescendo is

Track 95

Open String Shading

Adagio
arco

Track 96

Slur

Just like the tie, the **slur** is a curved line, which connects two notes. Unlike the tie, however, the **slur** connects notes that are different in pitch. Notes connected by a slur are played together in the same bow. The slur creates a smooth and connected sound.

Brahms (1833-1897), a German composer and pianist during the Romantic era, is one of the most notable composers not only of his time, but also in the entire course of music history. His music was traditional, yet innovative. Grouped alongside Bach and Beethoven as one of "The Three Bs," Brahms experienced considerable popularity during his life and music career.

Track 97

Symphony #1

Moderato
arco

Fermata = hold note longer than usual

Brahms

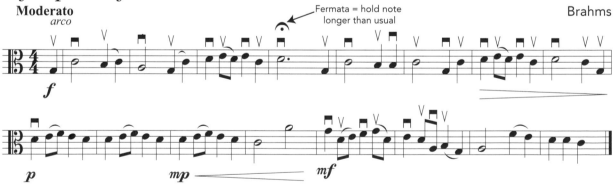

Track 98

Amazing Grace

Andante

Articulation (Staccato and Legato)

Articulation refers to performance techniques, which affect not only the sound of a single note, but also the flow between groups of notes. The slur is a type of musical articulation. Different bow strokes also serve as musical articulations. Two basic bow articulations are **staccato** and **legato**.

Staccato is denoted by a dot (·), which is placed above the note head. To perform staccato, keep the bow on the string and play the notes short and detached.

Legato is notated with a long dash (−), which is placed above the note head. To create a legato feeling, play the note on the string with a long and smooth bow stroke. The slur is associated with the legato bow stroke.

Track 100

Open String Articulation

Bach, a Baroque era composer known for his intense chord progressions, is single-handedly one of the most influential composers and musicians in all of music history. His dance suites and organ music still hold tremendous importance in the music world. In this abbreviated version of Bach's "Minuet," watch for dynamics, and new bow articulations.

Track 101

Minuet by J.S. Bach

Bach

D.C. al Fine

D.C. al Fine, or **Da Capo al fine**, means from the head (or beginning) to the end. When you see D.C al fine, you will repeat to the beginning of the music and play through until you see the word **Fine**.

"Country Gardens" contains many repeated patterns. Identifying these will help you to learn the piece more quickly.

Country Gardens

"Caribbean Folk Song" is lively and fun to play. Some practice steps you may find useful include:

- Look at the music before playing, noticing every mark and symbol.
- Tap or clap the rhythm.
- Play pizzicato first to become familiar with the notes.
- Look ahead for slurs before bowing.

Caribbean Folk Song

Now that you have put it all together, it's time to enjoy some duets with a friend. Find a performance buddy and bask in the fruits of your hard labor!

Track 102

Ode to Joy

Beethoven

Track 103

When the Saints Go Marching In

Traditional

Boatman Dance

Joyous

American Folk Song

Fingering Chart

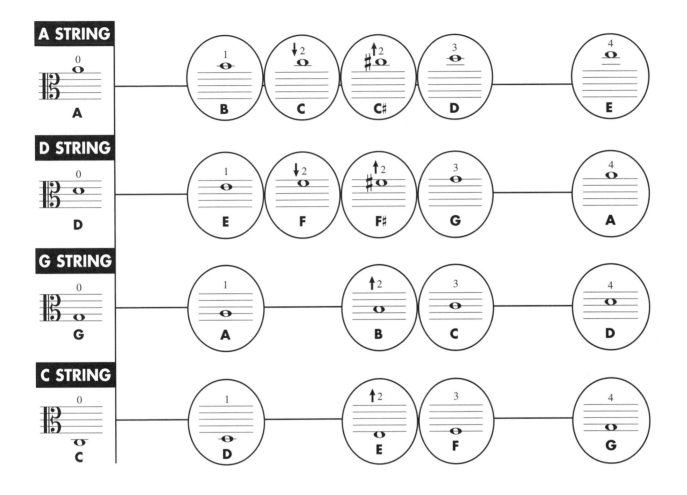

Maintenance and Accessories

To keep your viola and bow in good condition, you will need a case. Before putting your viola and bow away in its case, always wipe them down thoroughly. When cleaning the bow, you should wipe the stick, but not the bow hairs. From time to time, polish the instrument to keep it looking beautiful! To protect the wood of the instrument from cracking, keep a viola humidifier in the case during the cold months of the year.

Below is a list of recommended accessories for maintenance. These items will help you achieve your best performance on the viola!

- Rosin

- Humidifier

- Cleaning and Polishing Cloth

- Instrument polish and cleaner

- Spare set of strings: because strings tend to break at the most inconvenient times.

- Metronome: you will use this later on in the book to help you keep tempo.

- Shoulder Rest: this attaches underneath the viola at the base and is a crucial aid for holding the viola properly with more ease.

- Tuner: until you are confident using the system of fifths to tune your open strings, you will need either a keyboard or a tuner. The book also includes an audio sample of the open strings, which you can use to tune.

    *To match non-open string notes, a tuner is recommended. There are several types of tuners available. Some tuners play a specific note of your choice, allowing you to audibly match the pitch. Other tuners, common among guitar players, clip onto the scroll of the viola. Instead of sounding the pitch for you to match, you play the pitch and a needle moves to indicate whether you need to raise or lower your pitch.

- Music Stand: this holds your music at the proper angle and height so that you do not have to strain your neck and back.

Glossary of Musical Terms

Accent	Place extra emphasis on the note.
Accidental	Any natural (♮), sharp (♯), or flat (♭), sign that is in the music, but does not appear in the key signature.
Adagio	Tempo marking - play very slowly.
Allegro	Tempo marking - play fast.
Alto Clef	𝄡 Designates the middle line of the staff as the note C, also called the C clef.
Andante	Play at a slower "walking" tempo.
Arco	Play by drawing the bow.
Bar Lines	Lines used to divide the staff into musical segments called measures.
Beat	The steady pulse throughout a piece of music.
Breath Mark	' Shows where to take a breath in the music, as well as lift, or retake, the bow.
Common Time	𝄴 This is a also known as 4/4 time signature.
Crescendo	Gradually louder.
D.C. al Fine	Play through until you see D.C. al Fine in the music, then repeat to the beginning and play through until you see Fine.
Decrescendo	Gradually quieter.
Dotted Note	When a dot is added to any note, it increases the duration of the original value by half.
Double Bar Line	Indicates the end of a piece.
Down-bow	⊓ Draw the bow downward towards the ground.
Dynamics	Markings which indicate how loud (f) or soft (p) to play.
Duration	The amount of time assigned to a rhythmic value.
Eighth Note	♪ Half the value of a quarter note; two or more can be joined by a beam: ♫ Two eighth notes equal one quarter note.
Eighth Rest	♪ Half the value of a quarter rest. Two eighth rests equal one quarter rest.
Fermata	⌢ Hold the note or rest for longer than its notated value. .
Flat	♭ Lowers a note a half step.
Forte	f Play loudly.
Half Note	♩ Receives two beats of sound and is equal to two quarter notes.
Half Rest	▬ Two beats of silence; equal to two quarter rests.
Interval	The distance between two pitches.
Key Signature	Denotes which pitches to play throughout an entire piece of music.
Ledger Lines	Small lines placed above or below the staff, which extend the range of the normal musical staff. Ledger lines allow for notes to be placed above or below the lines and spaces of the regular musical staff.
Legato	— Long, smooth bow strokes.
Measure	Space between two bar lines containing the number of beats determined by the time signature.
Mezzo Forte	mf Play medium loud.
Mezzo Piano	mp Play medium soft.
Moderato	A moderate tempo.

Natural	♮ Cancels a previous sharp or flat.
Notes	Symbols that, when placed on a music staff, tell the player which notes to play.
Octave	Distance from one note to eight notes higher or lower (in the same key).
Phrase	A musical sentence, which can be two or more measures long.
Piano	*p* Play quietly.
Pick-up Notes	One or more notes before the first full measure, also called upbeats or anacrusis.
Pitch	The highness or lowness of a note, which is indicated by its horizontal placement on the staff.
Pizzicato	*pizz.* means to pluck the string rather than bow it.
Quarter Note	♩ Receives one beat of sound. There are 4 quarter notes in a 4/4 measure and 3 in a 3/4 measure.
Quarter Rest	𝄽 Receives one beat of silence.
Repeat Sign	:‖ Repeat a section, or entire piece of music.
Rests	Symbols that represent silence.
Rhythm	Duration of notes and rests.
Scale	A sequence of notes in ascending or descending order.
Sharp	♯ Raises a note a half step.
Slur	A curved line, which connects two or more notes that are played in the same bow.
Staccato	Notes played with a short and detached articulation.
Staff	Five horizontal lines and four spaces; note placement on the staff determines how high or low the note will sound.
Subdivision	Breaking a larger rhythmic unit down into smaller segments in order to understand more complex rhythms.
Tempo	The speed designated for a piece of music.
Tie	A curved line connecting two notes of the same pitch. A tie between the notes gives the first note the value of both notes "tied" together.
Time Signature	Placed at the beginning of a piece of music, the time signature indicates how many beats per measure and what type of note receives one beat.
Up-bow	V Pushing the bow upwards, towards the ceiling.
Whole note	𝅝 Lasts four beats, or a complete measure in 4/4 time.
Whole Rest	▬ Equals 4 beats of silence, or a complete measure of silence in 4/4 time.